TINNEL GODS

by Fiona Whitelaw

‖ SAMUEL FRENCH ‖

samuelfrench.co.uk

FOR AMATEUR PRODUCTION ENQUIRIES

UNITED KINGDOM AND WORLD EXCLUDING NORTH AMERICA
plays@SamuelFrench-London.co.uk
020 7255 4302/01
UNITED STATES AND CANADA
info@SamuelFrench.com
1-866-598-8449
Each title is subject to availability from Samuel French, depending upon country of performance.

Cover photograph © Martin Shakeshaft - www.strike84.co.uk

THINKING ABOUT PERFORMING A SHOW?

There are thousands of plays and musicals available to perform from Samuel French right now, and applying for a licence is easier and more affordable than you might think

---

From classic plays to brand new musicals, from monologues to epic dramas, there are shows for everyone.

Plays and musicals are protected by copyright law so if you want to perform them, the first thing you'll need is a licence. This simple process helps support the playwright by ensuring they get paid for their work, and means that you'll have the documents you need to stage the show in public.

Not all our shows are available to perform all the time, so it's important to check and apply for a licence before you start rehearsals or commit to doing the show.

LEARN MORE & FIND THOUSANDS OF SHOWS

Browse our full range of plays and musicals and find out more about how to license a show
www.samuelfrench.co.uk/perform

Talk to the friendly experts in our Licensing team for advice on choosing a show, and help with licensing
plays@samuelfrench.co.uk   020 7387 9373

Acting Editions

BORN TO PERFORM

Playscripts designed from the ground up to work the way you do in rehearsal, performance and study

---

Larger, clearer text for easier reading

Wider margins for notes

Performance features such as character and props lists, sound and lighting cues, and more

---

+ CHOOSE A SIZE AND STYLE TO SUIT YOU

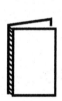

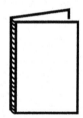

STANDARD EDITION	SPIRAL-BOUND EDITION	LARGE EDITION
Our regular paperback book at our regular size	The same size as the Standard Edition, but with a sturdy, easy-to-fold, easy-to-hold spiral-bound spine	A4 size and spiral bound, with larger text and a blank page for notes opposite every page of text. Perfect for technical and directing use

LEARN MORE | **samuelfrench.co.uk/actingeditions**

TINNED GOODS

TOUR DATES

11 March, Brindley Studio, Runcorn
12 March, Salford Arts Theatre
18 March, mac Birmingham
19 March, Artrix, Bromsgrove
24 March, Storey Theatre, Lancaster
30 March, Greenwich Theatre
31 March, Garrick Theatre, Lichfield
1 April, Nottingham Arts Theatre
2 April, Unity 2, Liverpool
3 April, Arcola Theatre, London

ABOUT THE AUTHOR

Theatre includes: *Acceptable Damage* Angelic Tales Theatre Royal Stratford, *Chosen* Home Theatre UK Theatre Royal Stratford, *Clearance* (commissioned by Lumenis Theatre and performed Southwark Playhouse, Old Red Lion, Camden People's Theatre) also performed Mind The Gap Theater NYC, *Walker* Mind The Gap Theater NYC, *Separate Reality* Just Jones, *Let A Smile Be Your Umbrella* (10 forum plays commissioned by Central & Cecil). *42 Days* Teatro Vivo, *Think It True & If You Were Cecil* GLYPT, *A Visit To The Launderette* Sydenham Arts Festival.

Film: Acceptable Damage feature in post production. Currently under commission for a second feature.

AUTHOR'S NOTE

All of us who lived through the 80s remember the havoc wreaked on the trade union movement by the Thatcher government. Not least the deliberate targeting of the NUM and the destruction of the mining industry in the UK with the resulting decline in those communities and towns that lost their livelihoods.

The Women Against Pit Closures march in August 1984 was and still is the largest female protest recorded. The women who joined this movement found their lives transformed as they gained a political voice and released unlocked skills, potential for leadership and a passion to protect the rights of their sisterhood and families.

It is for these women I wrote the play to celebrate their graft and generosity of spirit. To give voice to a story that is often told from a male point of view. As one of the audience at our show at Lichfield Garrick said, "We don't want to be just a paragraph in the history books".

It is also for the generation of women who follow after, so that they will know what went before, honour it and learn from these women. We all have a voice, and we can all use it.

**FIONA WHITELAW AND TEA AND TENACITY WOULD LIKE TO
THANK**

Liz Bagley. Sarah Berger of The So and So Arts Club

ABOUT TEA AND TENACITY

Tea and Tenacity performs new work that provokes discussion, represents the female voice and experience and aims to create opportunities for Midlands-based artists. We would welcome your feedback.

Please visit us online and say hello at

@TeaTenacity

www.facebook.com/TeaandTenacity

www.teaandtenacity.co.uk

We are extremely grateful for receiving support and funding from the following organisations: **Arts Council England, Unite the Union, Sir Barry Jackson Trust and SERTUC.**

THE COMPANY

Rachel **Caroline Frewin**
Charlene **Jade Samuels**
Brenda **Jenny Stokes**
Bethany **Laura M Tipper**
Sue **Fiona Whitelaw**

Directed by **Alison Belbin**
Stage Managed by **Rob McNally** and **Zoe Carrico**
Theatre designed by **Zoe Rolph**

Caroline Frewin

Drawn to playing strong and complex characters, Caroline's recent work has included playing German scientist Dr Clara Immerwahr in the Arts Council funded *Home Fires Burning* and the survivor of domestic abuse in a charity film for Safeline. A runner up in the Norman Beaton Fellowship she has also worked with BBC Radio Drama, Birmingham Rep and RSC.

Jade Samuels

Jade is a proud alum of Rose Bruford's Acting course. Since graduating some of her credits include the musical *The Good Enough Mums Club*, appearing as episode guest lead in BBC's *Doctors*, and winning the 3 Minute round of Triforce Promotions 'Monologue slam'. She's thrilled to be involved with an all-female cast and a Midlands-based theatre company!

Jenny Stokes

Jenny has credits for TV, short film and stage, recently playing Gracie in *Holding Baby* by Jan Watts at the mac, Birmingham; Mrs Hanning, in comedy horror, *Cannibals and Carpet Fitters* (winner 2014 dead shorts) and Brenda in *Aston Telling Tales* directed by Ali Belbin (Women and Theatre). She has devised and performed her comedic alter ego, Dolly Grip at comedy festivals around the country.

Laura M Tipper

A recent graduate of renowned Ecole Philippe Gaulier in Paris, Laura is delighted to perform with Tea and Tenacity. Whilst training at Gaulier Laura played Sophocles' Electra, Shakespeare's Cleopatra and Nina in Chekhov's *The Seagull*. A lover of improvisation she recently devised Person Birds with Maison Foo and toured a physical theatre production with Highly Sprung Performance Company.

Fiona Whitelaw
Theatre credits include *Muncitor* for Theatre Royal Stratford East, *The Knitting Circle* in a national tour for Vital Xposure, *Love on the Dole* for Finborough Theatre, *Asylum Monologues* for Sheffield Crucible and *More Soup and Tart*, for the Barbican. Television work includes *Tales from the Old Bailey – The Suffragettes'* and *Princess and the Pea* for BBC2.

Director – Alison Belbin
Ali has worked across television, radio and theatre as an actress and in theatre also as a director. She played Maggie in three episodes of the BBC Drama series *Doctors* and directed *Other* by Lorna Laidlaw for a Midlands tour in October 2014. She also wrote and performed a one-woman play for Sandwell Women's Aid in Spring 2015 and co-wrote *Marks* (about self harm) for Women & Theatre which she also directed.

Stage Manager – Robert McNally is a recent graduate from Birmingham School of Acting. He has been fortunate enough to work on a variety of productions since graduating including *Brummegem Pals* (DSM) *In the Night Garden Live* (ASM) and *The Father*. (ASM)

Designer – Zoe Rolph is a Worcester-based theatre designer. She designed Tea and Tenacity's debut production, *First Do No Harm* as well as shows for Tread the Boards in Stratford Upon Avon (*Sense and Sensibility, Present Laughter, Aladdin*).

Dedicated to the women of The North Staffordshire Miners Wives Action Group and all the women involved in the dispute.

CHARACTERS

SUE – wife of a striking miner, forty-five
BETHANY – Sue's daughter, sixteen
CHARLENE – Bethany's best friend, sixteen
RACHEL – wife of a working miner, forty-six
BRENDA – Rachel's aunt, seventies
DON, PICKETS, POLICE, WORKING MINERS, and all other roles played by the company.

The play is set in a mining community during the strike of 1984-85.

The set is a kitchen that has been deconstructed and ripped apart, doors are hanging off cupboards and the cupboards are empty apart from a few cans of basic goods. Sides of cupboards can be removed to construct barricades, vehicles or other locations.

There is a table centre stage which is used for kitchen, police station and vehicle scenes. Rubble surrounds the outer edges of the stage: bricks, cardboard boxes, placards, truncheons, shields, objects for making Foley sound effects. Possibly the shields are not actual shields, but plastic dustbin lids to represent the "short shields" used by the Met police at the time.

ACT I

Scene One

It is early evening Friday 3rd August 1984 in SUE's *house. She is sitting at the kitchen table piling cans of food into a pyramid; there is a cardboard box next to them and a packet of Smash. She is totally focused on the task.*

We can see RACHEL *outside the back door holding three Sainsbury's bags. She hesitates.*

SUE *rearranges the cans and then sweeps them off the table, she puts every last ounce of energy into the task.*

RACHEL *hears the noise, concern overrides her hesitation and she tries the door. It is open, she puts the shopping bags down, enters.*

They look at each other.

This is both a familiar and totally new situation.

Silence. RACHEL *looks around.*

SUE They've taken the telly away, we couldn't make the payments.

RACHEL ...I know yer door always used to be open gone tea time, but I didn't...not any more...wasn't sure...

SUE Yesterday afternoon, in case yer curtains were twitching.

RACHEL They weren't.

SUE What do you want Rachel?

RACHEL I wouldn't, not at all, you know me?

SUE Do I? Now?

1

RACHEL The noise, I heard a right noise, just checkin' that yer alright?

SUE I'm alright.

RACHEL Don't say that, don't be like that.

SUE Like what?

RACHEL Well...

SUE On strike?

RACHEL You're not on strike.

SUE Am I not? Tell that to the kids when I've to give them this muck for their tea.

RACHEL I...

SUE Don't think me ungrateful, I am grateful for the parcels and all the nice bits they pop in, but what can I make with a tin of mince, some cherry pie filling and a packet of Smash.

RACHEL *(picking up a can)* There's peas.

SUE Oh well then, that sorts it then, the peas have saved the day.

RACHEL I just meant...

SUE You're livin' off a food parcel and it's Friday night so we'll be havin' our fish and chips and watching Blockbusters.

RACHEL No.

SUE BBC now is it?

RACHEL I didn't mean that, I wanted to *(beat)* I've been trying to come round for weeks and...

SUE Not trying very hard then.

RACHEL How would you know?

SUE You'd've made it. Two doors down, it's hardly an expedition. No need for your Datsun.

RACHEL You're making this hard.

SUE I'm making this hard? You made a choice and now you want me to make it easy for you.

RACHEL You made the choice, you stopped speaking to me.

SUE One hundred and fifty three days it's been since we came out.

RACHEL Since you drew a line down the street, made the school gates a battle zone.

SUE It is a war.

RACHEL But not against me, not with me, you're me mate, "Feathy Tech girls against the world".

SUE The world has changed.

RACHEL We're not "the world", we're us aren't we, still us, we can still be.

SUE Tell your Bob to come out on strike then.

RACHEL You know he's not going to do that, he thinks there should have been a ballot.

SUE That's old news, we are where we are.

RACHEL He can't afford to go on strike, it's not just us he's to support, there's the maintenance and...

SUE And you think Don can, do you think he likes me queuing up at the welfare and trying to feed his family on tinned good, hand-outs from strangers down south.

RACHEL No, I don't, I don't think he likes it, but I have to stand by Bob.

SUE You don't have an opinion of yer own then, can't think for yerself.

RACHEL I can, I do... I do think it's wrong, what the Coal Board is doing. I do, I...

SUE Then why don't you come with me on Saturday?

RACHEL Can we just, can we just speak?

SUE We're speaking.

RACHEL We're not, are we, you're still, you're making everything about the/

SUE The strike. Everything is about the strike, what the closures will do to us, to our families, our future, to the country, dividing us, splitting us, picking us apart.

RACHEL We're doing that for them aren't we? Not speaking to each other, making it about sides.

SUE You have to pick a side, you have picked a side.

RACHEL Sue, I haven't, you stopped speaking to me, remember, after they walked out, you, stopped, speaking, to, me.

SUE I didn't want to, it was necessary.

RACHEL Necessary, this wasn't a union resolution, we didn't hold a meeting. My mate just stopped speaking to me. My mate who I smoked me first fag with and told me how to clear up a love bite with toothpaste, my mate who saved her dad's records for me, my mate who held me hand when Roger didn't turn up for the birth and hid me for six weeks when I first left 'im. This mate, STOPPED SPEAKING TO ME.

SUE You have to see the banner, I'm going to get it and show yer.

RACHEL I don't want to see the bloody banner.

SUE Yer Aunty Brenda's worked up a whole section on it. Did you know?

RACHEL I didn't, no, we, I haven't seen her in a while.

SUE She only lives in the next street, you not speaking to her either?

RACHEL Bob says, with Uncle George being on strike and...

SUE So, you don't know she's been up the hospital for observations, she had a turn on the picket line, last Wednesday, they kept her in over night...

RACHEL *jumps.*

It's ok, she's back home, nothing to worry about.

RACHEL I didn't know, how would I.

SUE And I'm not speaking to you? You're not speaking to your Brenda.

RACHEL She stopped speak/

SUE You can remember can you, who stopped first, did you take minutes?

RACHEL I/

SUE So it is about the strike, how can it not be/

RACHEL I don't want it to be.

SUE But it is.

RACHEL I came round.

SUE Yes, why did you come round?

RACHEL Been trying to for weeks.

SUE You said.

RACHEL I've stood at yer door and wanted to... I couldn't face the, if you slammed it in my face and...

SUE You're inside now.

RACHEL Yes.

RACHEL *gets up and slowly walks to the door, opens it and brings in the three shopping bags, she puts them down beside the table. The two women hold each other's gaze.*

(Speaking very quickly, pushing the bags towards her with her foot) It's just a bit of a shop, not much, I've been getting a bit extra for you, when I go, and, and, I've sat out in the car, outside a few times and I didn't know how to say, how to give it to you, and I thought you'd take it the wrong way, I've brought it as far as the back door, but...but it's not meant to be, to be charity it's/

SUE Scab food/

RACHEL Take it for the kids... I miss seeing them... I see them across the street and...

SUE They look hungry?

RACHEL Bloody hell Sue.

SUE I can't, you know I can't, what would I say.

RACHEL Say you just got lucky this week in the food bank, I won't say anything.

SUE Someone might have seen you come in.

RACHEL They didn't.

SUE You can't be sure.

RACHEL It's not the Falls Road...

SUE Don't patronise me.

RACHEL You can tell them I was coming to say thanks for letting me know about Aunty Brenda. You mentioned it to me at the school gates and I came round to say thanks.

SUE Its not the best plan, it's hardly Juliet Bravo is it?

RACHEL It'll have to do...so, you can keep it, or leave it, or shove it in the bin, it's up to you, but I'm not taking it back... *(She moves towards the door, picks up the can of peas, puts it on the edge of the table)* I'll let meself out... *(She opens the door)*

SUE We're meeting at Gimhill car park at 5.30 next Saturday.

RACHEL leaves. SUE sits. (Beat) (She opens one of the bags, takes out a peach. She puts it up to her face, inhales, eyes closed. Gradually we hear the sound of "the strike" begin to surround her, figures step out of the shadows, their shouts are insistent and urgent.

PICKET 1 Here they come.

PICKET 2 Come on lads.

PICKET 3 Scab.

PICKET 2 Come out wi' us.

PICKET 3 Turn back.

PICKET 1 Scab, scab, scab, scab. *(Rising in volume)*

PICKET 2 Scaaaaaaab, scaaaaaab, scaaab. *(continuing)*

PICKET 3 Out, out, out. *(Continuing)*

The PICKETS circle SUE, not quite real, oppressive, she opens her eyes. Blackout.

Scene Two

Later the same afternoon **BETHANY** *and* **CHARLENE** *are leaning over the wall outside the entrance to the pit, their elbows are on the top of the wall, we only see their arms and faces, they are trying not to be noticed as they look down at* **PICKETS** *and* **POLICE** *below.*

BETHANY Gum?

CHARLENE Ta.

BETHANY Got any fags?

CHARLENE Three.

BETHANY Give us one then.

CHARLENE We'll 'ave to share.

BETHANY Why?

CHARLENE I'm keeping me last two for when I see Neil/

BETHANY Me boyfriend. Need them fer after do yer.

CHARLENE Don't be dirty.

BETHANY I'm not, fuck is a beautiful word, that's what Sir says.

CHARLENE What would he say that for.

BETHANY We're doing D H Lawrence, it's what 'e said.

Beat.

CHARLENE I never said we was doing it, did I.

BETHANY You didn't deny it though.

CHARLENE Bog off!

BETHANY Oooo Neil, just there, ooo go on.

CHARLENE Stop it or I'm going.

7

Beat. **BETHANY** *takes off her zipped top, she has a low cut t-shirt underneath.* **CHARLENE** *stares.*

What are we doing 'ere? If I wanted to stare at a bunch of miners scuffing their boots and talking bollocks, I could go down the welfare.

BETHANY There'd be no point; no one's got any money to buy you a drink.

CHARLENE Who would buy you a drink any road, not with yer dad watchin' on.

BETHANY There 'e is.

CHARLENE Who is?

BETHANY That one with the moustache.

CHARLENE None of them 'as a moustache. I thought you were bringin' me to see yer fella, and we ended up here!

BETHANY He's not me fella yet.

CHARLENE So which one is it?

BETHANY Him. *(She points)* The tall one.

CHARLENE The cop! Bloody 'ell...bloody 'ell...

BETHANY Why YOU so bothered, thought you were fed up of the strike.

CHARLENE Bloody hell...

BETHANY Alright, I get the point... He is gorgeous though isn't he; look at his arse in that uniform.

CHARLENE Is that it, the uniform? You can moon around the fire station fer that.

BETHANY It's not the uniform.

CHARLENE How long's this been going on?

BETHANY There's nowt goin' on...yet...

Beat.

I saw him when he came round to escort Bob Mathers to work, that time after they'd put stuff through 'is letter box and that, he came a few times, you must've seen.

CHARLENE I don't know, I might've done, they all look the same to me, them "white shirts", I don't look at them.

BETHANY Are you sure, they live next door to you. I wanted to know if he were wearin' a wedding ring.

She pulls out a notebook with a biro clipped on, it contains a newspaper clipping and the front of a cigarette packet stuck in. Dates and notes next to them.

CHARLENE What are you, 'is fan club?

BETHANY It's all the times I've seen 'im.

CHARLENE He's not in a band.

BETHANY 'E could be, 'e's got the looks.

CHARLENE He's not a boy.

BETHANY He's got a lovely deep voice.

CHARLENE I bet you've never spoken to him.

BETHANY I've walked past him, and stood near...by the brazier, when I've taken me dad some butties.

CHARLENE This has been going on a while then?

BETHANY Maybe.

CHARLENE You can't go with a rozzer.

BETHANY Do you think 'es fresh?

CHARLENE He's too old for you.

BETHANY But look at 'im, 'es is tasty, you have to admit it?

CHARLENE *(taking a long critical look)* He's alright. You should've brought yer dad's birdwatching binoculars if you'd wanted to make a proper assessment.

BETHANY I thought about it.

CHARLENE Bloody hell.

BETHANY Stop sayin' that.

Beat.

CHARLENE You can't. You can't go out with a rozzer, even if he weren't too old for you. You don't know what he's done.

BETHANY You mean who he's had?

CHARLENE No, what 'es done, on the picket line, with his truncheon or his bloody horse.

BETHANY He doesn't 'ave a horse, I don't think 'e does. I've always wanted to be carried off on horseback.

CHARLENE GET A GRIP. Them "white shirts" they're the mafia of the police, me dad says, them short shield units. You don't know what he's done, what 'e did at Orgreave. You can't be sure it wasn't 'im hit Billy Preston or put Tom what's 'is name in hospital, or split some other striker's bonce up. You don't know, and you won't know, even if you did 'ave a drink with him or whatnot. 'Cos it's a war 'in't it and 'es on't other side, and you'll never know, or never be sure.

BETHANY Do you 'ave to be so bloody serious, I just fancy 'im right.

CHARLENE This is serious, you can't just pretend strike's not 'appening.

BETHANY Don't I bloody know that, it's like campaign central round ours, banners and maps and...

CHARLENE Shit!

BETHANY What?

CHARLENE Yer dad's seen you, 'e just waved.

BETHANY Now who's swearing. I'll have to tell him I came to meet him, that'll definitely be worth a can of pop.

CHARLENE Daddy's little girl.

BETHANY I'm jammy me.

CHARLENE You going down then?

BETHANY I shall 'ave ter...praps I can get a better look at 'im while I'm down there.

CHARLENE You better be kiddin'.

BETHANY *jumps down out of sight.* **CHARLENE** *follows.*

Scene Three

Early evening the same day. SUE'*s kitchen.* SUE *is kneeling on the floor hammering nails into a placard, fixing it to a broomstick.* BETHANY *enters.*

BETHANY What's that smell?

SUE Chicken stew.

BETHANY Actual chicken?

SUE Actual chicken.

BETHANY Did you rob it/

SUE Don't be daft.

BETHANY Where did it come from?

SUE *places a bowl of soup on the table,* BETHANY *sits, tries it and then begins to eat quickly and hungrily.*

It's Ace Mum.

SUE A mate got me the bird. *(Beat)* Why you late?

BETHANY I went to meet me dad.

SUE You didn't bring 'im home then?

BETHANY He's gone to a meeting, summat about a coach to another pit, I dunno.

SUE Did he say what time he'd be back.

BETHANY *shrugs, she has finished the soup, takes the dish out and comes back.*

BETHANY Did you take the fence down for the fire Mum?

SUE Which fence?

BETHANY Front.

SUE Our front?

BETHANY Yes, the front fence.

SUE It's gone?

BETHANY I said didn't I.

SUE Were it there this morning?

BETHANY I don't know, I'm always half asleep of a morning.

SUE I've only been out the back today, the buggers, we're all in this together aren't we? Nowt to be done now, spilt milk an all.

Will you wash the pots, I need to finish these placards for Saturday.

BETHANY Can't Robbie do it?

SUE He's most likely at'meeting with yer dad.

BETHANY Flippin' strike.

SUE I'll not 'ave that in here.

BETHANY It's all we ever talk about.

SUE What else is there more pressing.

BETHANY I need a new bra.

SUE Again.

BETHANY It's what happens, they grow.

SUE Yes.

BETHANY Yes I can 'ave one. I saw a turquoise one in catalogue.

SUE Yes, I heard you, and no, unless we get one in a clothes parcel, I'll keep me eye out for your size. What do you reckon you are?

BETHANY That's disgustin'. I'm not havin' some pre-worn gear some beggar's cast out.

SUE Do you have a better idea?

BETHANY *(as she exits)* I just won't wear one then, proper women's lib, I'll be like one of the Greenham women, that'd suit you wouldn't it?

SUE You best grow yer armpit hair an 'all.

Scene Four

Night, the same day in SUE's *kitchen, she is asleep at the table.*

Around her shadowy figures of POLICEMEN, *banging on their riot shields with truncheons.*

POLICEMAN 1 Get back, back up, no further...

POLICEMAN 2 Put that down and there'll be no trouble.

POLICEMAN 3 I'm on £500 a week, hope the strike goes on longer...

POLICEMAN 2 How do you spend your picketing money?

POLICEMAN 1 Who's giving it one at home.
Get back.

POLICEMAN 3 £500.

POLICEMAN 2 Picketing money/

POLICEMAN 1 Back, back/

POLICEMAN 3 Overtime/

POLICEMAN 1 Money/

POLICEMAN 2 *(barking like a dog)*

POLICEMAN 3 Set them on.

POLICEMAN 1 Fucking miners.

POLICEMAN 3 *(barking like a dog)*

They are all running on the spot, banging their truncheons on their shields, shouting, roaring, barking.

POLICEMAN 1 Money.

POLICEMAN 2 Pickets.

POLICEMAN 3 Get back.

POLICEMEN 1, 2, 3

Back, back, back... *(Cont)*

The **POLICEMAN** *back away leaving one figure who has no shield,* **DON,** **SUE**'s *husband.*

He remains in shadow, we never see his face. He is holding an open packet of chocolate digestives. He puts them down on the table in front of **SUE** *with some force.*

DON Chocolate digestives.

SUE Don?

DON Since when can we buy chocolate digestives.

SUE They come in the parcel, we got lucky.

DON Fairy fuckin' godmother?

SUE Come again?

DON I've been in the cupboard, the fridge, there's all sorts.

SUE I told you, we got lucky, can I go up to bed now?

DON Yer a liar. *(Pulling a crumpled Sainsbury's bag out of his pocket)* A liar, we don't go to Sainsbury's, there's no money fer Sainsbury's.

SUE There's no money fer anything.

DON It was in the dustbin.

SUE Why were you going through the dustbin?

DON Chucking me chip wrapper, that's when I saw it.

SUE Chips! Excuse me fer givin' the kids chocolate biscuits.

DON I've not dipped into the money.

SUE Neither have I.

DON Then where's it from?

SUE I told you.

DON It doesn't come like that, it comes in a box.

Silence.

SUE One of the mums from school/

DON Which mum?

SUE Rachel.

DON Rachel? *(Beat)* Rachel.

Silence. He paces.

You brought scab food into this house.

SUE *(she is sitting up now)* I didn't bring it in, she brought it in.

DON You think that makes it better, SHE came into OUR house. You let a SCAB, bring SCAB food into our house.

SUE She's not a scab, it's her Bob who's not on strike not her, she most probably got it with her money, from her club wages, from her, it's not.

DON You can put that muck back into this bag and throw it in the bin.

SUE takes the Sainsbury's bag off him gently...

SUE Don. The kids are hungry, Don, they are going to bed hungry, teenagers need food, a lot of food, good food... I had to take it fer them, they had chicken fer their tea, first time in months and they bloody loved it, I put yours by for yer, when yer came back from the meeting, and... I didn't 'ave any meself, just gravy and the bread...and...

DON You must be hungry then, eh, best eat some of these *(banging the digestive packet down on the table)* musn't go to bed 'ungry lass.

SUE I'm keeping 'em fer the kids, I haven't had any, I won't.

DON But you must, have a taste of scab food, I'm sure it tastes better than what comes in't parcel.

SUE They're fer the kids.

DON Go on, *(he takes one out and pushes it into her hand)* 'ave a taste, 'ow long since you 'ad a choccy biccy? *(Leaning over her)* take a bite, go on, bite it, bite it...

SUE *reluctantly begins to eat the biscuit, she finishes, he watches.*

Are you enjoying it, or does it taste like the slag heap...well... well?

He takes another from the packet.

SUE No Don, one's enough.

DON It isn't though is it, if the kids are hungry you're hungry, you must be, you said yerself you didn't eat nothin' but the gravy.

SUE No, it's OK, I don't want another.

DON Yes, you do.

Put it in, put it in... Put it right in.

He puts another biscuit directly into her mouth.

The lights fade, BETHANY *walks in, stands frozen by the sink.* DON *doesn't see her. He drops the packet on the floor, exits upstairs.* BETHANY *picks up the packet. Blackout.*

Scene Five

Physical sequence of PICKETS *being manhandled by the* POLICE.

Hand or arm across the throat pulling a picket backwards. Pulling a picket along by the leg while they are standing. Carrying a picket face down by the arms and legs.

Using the following dialogue, the PICKETS *speak with the regional accents of many mining communities.*

This sequence of lines may be repeated in total or from "the full power of the state..." to suit the physical action.

PICKET 1 "They practised in Ireland, they practised in Brixton and Toxteth..."

PICKET 2 "when it came to our turn, they'd perfected their techniques"

PICKET 3 "they used them to great effect on us"

LAWYER "What is a riot?"

PICKET 3 "What is a riot?"

LAWYER "A riot is when three or more people, gather together, and have in their mind."

PICKET 1 "when it came to our turn."

LAWYER "a common purpose which they intend to achieve through force."

PICKET 2 "when it came to our turn."

PICKET 3 "when it came to our turn, they'd perfected their techniques."

PICKETS 1, 2, 3 "And used them to great effect on us."

PICKET 3 "The full power of the state is being used against workers in this dispute."

PICKET 2 "If you think it's only going to be used against—"

PICKET 1 "Miners—"

PICKET 2 "Industrial workers—"

PICKET 3 "People on peace protests—"

PICKET 2 "Students—"

PICKET 1 "Best open your eyes."

PICKET 2 "They may use it on anyone."

PICKET 1 "What is a riot?"

PICKET 2 "What is a riot?"

PICKET 3 "What is a riot?"

Scene Six

Saturday 4th August, late afternoon.

BRENDA *is seated at her kitchen table, she is stirring a batch of flapjack, one of her legs is up on a chair.*

BETHANY *(offstage)* Aunty Brenda, are you in?

BRENDA Is the door open?

BETHANY *(entering)* Yes.

BRENDA Guess I'm in then.

BETHANY You bakin' them right now?

BRENDA They're fer the march, if you want one, you'll have to come with.

BETHANY Mum keeps mithering me about it.

BRENDA With good reason, why would you not want to?

BETHANY I've got things to do.

BRENDA More important than this? More important than/

BETHANY Bringin' down the Thatcher government. Everbody talks in clichés at the moment, forgets about other stuff, there wasn't enough money for tampons last week and I'd to make do with cheapo pads, flippin disgusting it was; mince with smash on, mince with boil-in-the-bag rice from parcel, mince with mince.

BRENDA And you should be grateful for that, I was down at Greenham last month and there was almost nothing but/

BETHANY Mice cooked on a bonfire, I don't care, I'm sick of it, I am.

BRENDA Nobody eats mice.

BETHANY Probably bad karma or some such. Aunty Brenda, I'm dead serious. Me teenage years spent on grotty coach trips to coalfields and how to make 50p last a week at school.

BRENDA It only been months Bethany.

BETHANY Well they've felt like years.

BRENDA What's eatin' at you love?

She gets up taking the tray of flapjack, putting it in the oven. She is limping.

BETHANY Me mum told me you'd been hurt on't picket line, but I didn't think hurt, hurt.

BRENDA What other kind of hurt is there?

BETHANY She said you were alright.

BRENDA I am alright.

BETHANY So, how did you? How did...?

BRENDA Just bashed up a bit, I had a funny turn. I fell, they took me in overnight, a lot of stuff and nonsense, it'll take more than a police shove to keep me away.

BETHANY You will be careful though?

BRENDA Throw the first brick do you mean?

BETHANY I thought Scargill said his pickets didn't throw stuff.

BRENDA Nobody's on their best behaviour down there. And it's Mr Scargill to you lady.

BETHANY There's this bloke...

BRENDA *raises her eyebrows.*

Lad, there's this lad, and um...

BRENDA You like 'im. Is he sweet on you then?

BETHANY We haven't spoken yet.

BRENDA Why not?

BETHANY He's not from round here, I mean, he's only just moved in I think, and, um... I don't...

BRENDA Want to make first move. Well sometimes you have to love. Men can be a bit backward in coming forward.

BETHANY Yes, I know, but, he might not like me.

BRENDA You'll never know if you don't dip yer toe in the water.

BETHANY Me dad might not like him?

BRENDA Because he's a bloke, a bit older?

BETHANY Yes, that, and...

BRENDA 'Appen you can worry about that after you know if he's keen.

BETHANY I suppose.

BRENDA Best find some road to introduce yerself hadn't you. Is he a pit man?

BETHANY Surface I think.

BRENDA Less brass, but more chance of keepin' 'im. You'll think of summat.

Scene Seven

Monday 7th August.

As the scene slips from one place to another, we hear the picketing WOMEN *shouting at the* POLICE *and chanting.*

WOMEN Eff off back down south.

Pigs, pigs...

(chanting) Oh I'd rather be a picket than a scab,

I'd rather be a picket than a scab.

I'd rather be a picket,

I'd rather be a picket.

Rather be a picket than a scab.

Outside a pit, the women are edging their way through the crowd to get to the front, near the gates of the pit, as the action progresses they are each moved and shoved (shadowed) by a POLICE *officer that we can't see.*

We see SUE, BRENDA, BETHANY *and* CHARLENE, *it is the girls' first trip to the picket line.*

SUE Stick close by girls and don't get lost in't crowd.

BRENDA They're smart enough, teenagers these days have a lot more about them.

SUE Always moonin' about sayin' they're bored.

BRENDA No chance of that...oops 'ere we go...

The WOMEN *move forward as if swept on a wave.*

BETHANY It's like being on a rollercoaster.

SUE It's not Blackpool, make sure you stand yer ground.

CHARLENE I'm not sure, I think I might go back.

BRENDA You can't go back now love, there's no way through.

CHARLENE I feel sick.

BRENDA You'll be OK, once the vans come and you can start shouting properly.

SUE You got that camera Bethany?

BETHANY Yes Mum.

SUE Don't let them see it.

BETHANY I'll keep it in me pocket.

SUE You need it out, so you can get them at it.

BETHANY In me hand then.

CHARLENE Don't drop it, you've got those pictures on it remember.

BETHANY Ssssh.

CHARLENE How are you going to get those developed under 'er nose?

BETHANY I'll make sure I take it into't chemist.

CHARLENE You won't get away with that.

BETHANY I will, I can say I took it today can't I.

BRENDA Here it comes, come on girls. The first surge.

They reel and twist moving with the shoves and swings of batons, moving forwards and backwards. They can clearly see the **POLICE** *around them.*

SUE Scaaab.

BRENDA Come out and join us, we're stronger together.

SUE Turn back...scaab, scaaab.

BETHANY *(tentatively at first)* Scab.

CHARLENE Scab.

BETHANY AND CHARLENE Scab, scab, scab, scab.

BRENDA Turn back. Grab onto us girls.

SUE Turn back, turn back... Turn baaaaaack.

The **WORKING MINERS** *have gone through the pit gates, the women breathe out. Ahead of them, they see a* **POLICEMAN** *is charging towards a woman with his baton raised.*

BRENDA Watch it, you watch it, watch out.

SUE Whoaaa ooo shit.

The **WOMEN** *react to someone being hit.* **BETHANY** *has her camera and takes several pictures winding on the film. The* **WOMEN** *watch as a woman in front of them is struck to the ground.*

BETHANY Got it, got a brilliant shot of that.

BRENDA *(speaking to the injured woman)* Are you alright, you ok?

CHARLENE She's bleeding!

SUE Take a shot of 'im wi' 'is number covered up.

BETHANY Got it.

SUE Nice one, yer a dab 'and...

BETHANY Can I send it to the paper Mum, will they print it?

CHARLENE And a picture of us with it.

BETHANY Daily Mirror.

POLICE OFFICER 1 *(shouting)* Camera!

POLICE OFFICER 2 Camera!

SUE Get the film out, wind it on.

BETHANY What for?

SUE Get rid of evidence, them pickets threw bricks and we did nowt.

BRENDA Give it to me.

SUE Don't put yerself in the firing line.

BETHANY *passes the camera to* **BRENDA.**

BRENDA Chuck us another film Beth.

BETHANY It's not finished yet, there's more shots.

BRENDA *winds on the film, takes it out and shoves it in her bra.*

BRENDA Give us the new one.

BETHANY *passes it,* **BRENDA** *pops the new film in while keeping an eye out.*

POLICEMAN 1 Over there, one of them's got it.

POLICEMAN 2 Give me that camera.

BRENDA What for officer, shall we have us picture taken, "a day out in Nottingham".

POLICEMAN 2 Give it over.

BRENDA Didn't they teach you manners down south?

POLICEMAN 2 *(grabbing her arm)* Give me the camera.

She throws the camera, the women pass it between them, fun but menace all the same. **CHARLENE** *ends up with it, the* **POLICEMAN** *twists her arm up her back.*

SUE Leave off her, she's just a kid.

POLICEMAN 2 Give me the camera. *(He wrenches the camera out of her fingers, opens it up, pulls out the film and throws it)*

BRENDA Nice one lasses, you alright Charlene, saw a bit of action on yer first day out.

CHARLENE Bit frightening and a bit exiting.

SUE S'long as yer not too shook up.

Scene Eight

Tuesday 8th August, early morning 6 am. A soup kitchen, the striking women are setting up for the day to feed the **PICKETS** *and other striking family members.*

The roles of **SHIRLEY** *and* **DERA** *are played by the actors playing* **CHARLENE** *and* **BETHANY**.

SHIRLEY Let's get this corned beef kitchen up and running then.

BRENDA Are we disguising it today or serving it "à la mode"?

SHIRLEY Best not send you down to London too many times.

BRENDA Just means as it comes.

SHIRLEY *(holding up a thumb with extensive plasters on)* It comes in branded thumb slicing device, that's one thing I do know.

DERA Yesterday?

SHIRLEY Dog tired, all me chores at home to do when I finish here.

BRENDA Yesterday were fritters.

SHIRLEY Tuesday we did Argentinean pie with carrots.

This raises a laugh with the women.

BRENDA Monday were stew.

DERA Hash it is then.

> **DERA** *grabs a pan and starts opening cans, the others chop.* **RACHEL** *enters at the very edge of their space.*

SHIRLEY You can't come in 'ere.

RACHEL I only want to speak to Bren/

SHIRLEY Well you can't, whatever it is. We don't 'ave scabs in 'ere.

RACHEL I just came to speak to Brenda.

27

DERA *(standing in front of her)* She don't want to speak to a scab.

RACHEL Can I ask her, she's only there?

SHIRLEY *(banging the side of a saucepan with a spoon in time)* NO. YOU. CAN'T.

RACHEL Please, I heard she/was ill.

DERA *(joining in with the banging, a colander and a metal spoon)* SCABS OUT. SCABS OUT. SCABS OUT...

RACHEL Please, I please...

DERA SCABS OUT. SCABS OUT.

SHIRLEY OUT. OUT.

DERA OUT. OUT.

They both continue until...

BRENDA Alright girls. She can speak to me outside. *(To RACHEL)* Follow me. *(Takes her by the arm, walks her out, we can still see them)*

Do you want to get yerself slapped?

Beat.

You've got some balls I'll give you that.

RACHEL I heard you'd been taken ill. I couldn't not...

BRENDA You can see I'm still in one piece, best not hang around here if you want to stay the same.

RACHEL They won't hurt me, they know I'm yer family.

BRENDA Feelings are running pretty high.

RACHEL Blood's thicker than water isn't it?

BRENDA I wouldn't be so sure, right about now, it's getting pretty biblical.

Beat.

RACHEL I wanted to ask you something. *(Beat)* Do you think we'll win.

BRENDA We?

RACHEL The miners.

BRENDA WE have to.

RACHEL 'Cos it doesn't seem right, you, well, fighting for everything that's important to me, and me, me. I don't know what I'm doing.

BRENDA What are you doing?

RACHEL Dropping off clothes to welfare at night, leaving food at the foodbank with a headscarf on, reading a copy of The Miner behind Bob's back.

BRENDA You can't be half and half, you're either on strike or you're not.

RACHEL I'm still working at the club, we're not on strike.

BRENDA I know that Rachel, but if you're going to support us, then it has to be all the way, not half measures.

RACHEL But half of me is with you, and half with Bob.

BRENDA Then you need to know which half has the upper hand.

RACHEL How can I tell?

BRENDA Test it out, test your mettle by coming out somewhere you're not known.

RACHEL A flying picket.

BRENDA Speaking to those who haven't joined the fight, just talkin' to them. I'm off after I've got the hash on, getting a ride with a taxi man, he's been very sympathetic to the cause, takin' us down to Notts and doing his drivin' at night.

RACHEL You think that's the answer?

BRENDA It's the way to find an answer.

RACHEL It'll cost me a day's pay if I call in now.

BRENDA Small price to pay for the truth.

Scene Nine

Later the same day. BRENDA *and* RACHEL *are manning a protest in a supermarket car park, they have placards in a trolley and a picnic table with stickers, a petition, a collecting tin. They are stopping women as they come out of the shop, asking for donations to take back. A* MINER'S WIFE *passes and drops a few coins into the tin.* BRENDA *calls after her.*

BRENDA Just stop and have a chat love, we just want to explain things, why we've come down to see you.

NOTTS MINER'S WIFE I've put some money in yer tin.

BRENDA Stop and have a word, you've time before pickin' up yer kiddies I'm sure.

> NOTTS MINER'S WIFE *scurries past. A woman passes them with her bags and drops some things into the trolley.*

We just want a few minutes, to tell you how it's going, why we need your support.

We can defeat the NCB if we're all in, it'll be over quick if we're united.

> NOTTS MINER'S WIFE *turns and speaks from a safe distance.*

NOTTS MINER'S WIFE I'll give yer two minutes, I've things to do.

BRENDA I do appreciate it, I know yer in a difficult position.

NOTTS MINER'S WIFE Not as difficult as yours.

BRENDA True enough, but we do appreciate yer support.

> RACHEL *is rattling the money tin and giving out leaflets.*

NOTTS MINER'S WIFE Let's 'ave it then, I haven't got all day.

BRENDA It's a simple matter, isn't it. We want to win this strike, not just for our men, but for our community. The men might say it's only women, but look at what we've done. Feeding folk on every picket line, collecting clothing, seeing where need is and finding a way through, travelling to picket line and still turning up for our job (if we have one). We're not just here to beg for food but to fight for a cause. This morning two of your men turned back at the gates, think on that, they know we've right on our side. This government's trying to starve us back to work, but they won't do it. All I'm asking is that you talk about it at home, think of the power us women have.

NOTTS MINER'S WIFE, *digs into her bag and puts a decent can of ham into the trolley.*

NOTTS MINER'S WIFE I can't say I'll do it, but I'm glad I met you, I am.

They hug, she almost runs away with her bags/trolley.

RACHEL How do you do it?

BRENDA I don't know meself, I open me mouth and out it comes.

RACHEL Not sure I could.

BRENDA You are, yer here aren't you.

Other women wander past

RACHEL *(loudly)* Give to the striking miners! Women against pit closures!

BRENDA Stop and have a chat.

RACHEL Food for the striking miners.

Two **POLICE OFFICERS** *approach. They grab* **RACHEL** *and march her off, her feet almost off the floor.*

BRENDA Why are you arresting her, she's done nothing?

They lift her onto the table as if putting her into a police van.

POLICEMAN 1 You can put her in as well.

BRENDA What for, what have I done? Just defending our jobs, we are, leave off, I can climb in by meself.

The POLICE OFFICER 1 *pushes her into the van, she falls, he picks her up and almost throws her onto the table.*

RACHEL Now what do we do?

BRENDA Sit tight, they've nothing on us, they'll 'ave to let us go.

RACHEL I don't understand, we were just talking to people, I don't understand.

BRENDA They don't need a reason love, I've learned that much in the past few months.

RACHEL I need the toilet.

BRENDA Try and stay calm.

The OFFICERS *pull them from the back of the* "van" RACHEL *runs, the* WPC *runs and manhandles her into another* "cell". POLICE OFFICER 1 *pulls* BRENDA *roughly onto a chair and sits opposite her.*

POLICE OFFICER 1 Name please?

BRENDA Margaret Thatcher.

POLICE OFFICER 1 Tell me your name and address.

BRENDA Margaret Thatcher, 10 Downing Street, Westminster/ London.

WPC Get undressed please.

RACHEL Why? Why do I have to do that?

WPC Get undressed.

POLICE OFFICER 1 What newspaper do you read?

BRENDA Pravda.

POLICE OFFICER 1 I said what newspaper?

BRENDA It IS a newspaper... What do you read, The Beano?

POLICE OFFICER 1 The Daily Express.

BRENDA That figures.

WPC Take off your jumper and skirt please.

RACHEL What for?

WPC I am searching for offensive weapons and drugs.

RACHEL Why do I have to do that, I were just handing out leaflets.

WPC Take off your jumper and skirt.

RACHEL Would you like someone doing this to your mum?

WPC I'm only doing my job.

RACHEL Or yer grandma, or/yer aunty.

POLICE OFFICER 1 What do you think of Arthur Scargill?

BRENDA He's the NUM president.

POLICE OFFICER 1 What do you think of him?

BRENDA Arthur Scargill is the president of the National Union Of Mineworkers.

WPC Take off your shoes and give them to me.

RACHEL I'm not walking round here with no shoes on, there could be 'owt on this floor.

WPC Take them off.

RACHEL takes them off. **WPC** *takes the laces out of the shoes and gives them back to her.*

You can put your shoes back on.

RACHEL puts back on her shoes.

POLICE OFFICER 1 What newspaper do you read?

BRENDA I told you.

POLICE OFFICER 1 What's your opinion of Arthur Scargill? How would you describe your political views?

BRENDA Strongly held thank you very much.

POLICE OFFICER 1 Which way did you vote in the last election?

BRENDA How is this relevant to handing out some leaflets?

POLICE OFFICER 1 Tell me your name and address?

BRENDA You tell me yours.

RACHEL Why have you arrested me, I was only giving out leaflets.

POLICE OFFICER 1 How would you describe your political views? How did you vote in the last election?

WPC Take off your clothes.

RACHEL *(in tears)* I don't understand... I don't understand.

The **POLICE** *move back, leaving* **RACHEL** *and* **BRENDA** *standing alone in single spotlights.*

Scene Ten

The next day, Wednesday 9th August, morning. **BRENDA** *is finishing her breakfast.,* **BETHANY** *comes in, shouting through the door as usual but this time with some urgency.*

BETHANY *(offstage)* Aunty Brenda, are you in?

BRENDA Is the door open?

BETHANY *(entering slightly out of breath)* Yes.

BRENDA Guess I'm in then.

BETHANY I came round yesterday, three times, you were out.

BRENDA I was, that.

BETHANY Minto, next door, said you were gone down to Notts.

BRENDA He was right fer once.

BETHANY But then, you weren't back, when I called back, I mean, I came back at 9.30...

BRENDA I was very kindly put up fer the night.

BETHANY I thought Notts weren't out?

BRENDA Not the Notts, the local police very kindly put me in a cell fer the night.

BETHANY Arrested? Are you hurt?

BETHANY *comes close and looks at her, holds her hands.*

BRENDA *(she shakes her head)* If it hadn't happened to me, I shouldn't have credited it, I was always brought up to be respectful of the local copper, I thought you could reason with 'em, that's how I got stuck in the van, just asking why they'd put Rachel in, her first time on't picket line, frightening the life out of her. You hear about what's done to coloured people don't you, and I used to think, well, where there's smoke there's fire,

35

but Friday, after that, well, it bloody scared me I can tell you. It's like being in a police state. *(Staring very hard at* BETHANY*)* What's the rush to see me?

BETHANY Oh... I promised I'd take the film in, to develop it, in town, 'cos you're busy with the campaign...and...

BRENDA *(sitting)* It's been done already.

BETHANY Oh.

BRENDA You got some nice shots, of everything, very clear.

BETHANY The woman being hit?

BRENDA Yes, nice and sharp, and a very good one of you and the OTHER police officer *(beat)* the one with the moustache.

The striking MINERS *on the edge of the playing area begin to chant.*

MINERS 1 2 AND 3 The miners united will never be defeated. The miners united will never be defeated. The miners united will never be defeated.

Increasing in volume, lights fade.

ACT II

Scene One

Midday, the same day.

BETHANY is standing in a phone box, she has a handful of coins, she dials, counts to herself...

BETHANY *(mouthing silently)* One, two, three. *(She puts the receiver down, dials again, counts, mouthing silently)* One, two, three. *(She puts the receiver down, dials again, counts, mouthing silently)* One, two, three. *(She puts the receiver down, dials again, hears the beeps, pushes a coin in)*

Hello, hello, damn it. *(Slams the receiver down, she dials again, hears the beeps, pushes another coin in)* Hello, hello, go in damn it...yes it's me, who else would it be... No it's not cut off, we can't use it, the bill...didn't want 'er to 'ear anyroad, she was in, she's never in. *(Hears another beep, feeds another coin in)* Damn, I've got three more coins, so just listen...yes of course you can, where are you going?... At the social?... That'll be lame... Listen will yer. I need to borrow stuff, will you remember or do you need to write it down?... It's three things...right, your sleeping bag...the one you had fer Guide camp, do you still 'ave it...look then. Some money, whatever you can... I dunno...yes, do you think they'll notice? Your pac a mac. *(She puts in another coin)* It got ripped on't picket line... That A-Z yer mum got when she went down London...yes I know that's four things, you can remember four things can't you... Tonight, by the roundabout...the big one... eight-thirty... just promise will yer...no, I know you won't.

Scene Two

Wednesday 8th August. It is early afternoon. Open park or woodland near the village. SUE *is seated on a tree stump, she has a shopping bag, she takes out a flask, pours herself a drink. Waiting. A minute passes, she drinks.*

RACHEL *enters, sits down beside* SUE. *Silence.*

SUE Brew?

RACHEL May as well.

SUE I put sugar in.

RACHEL Is it an emergency?

SUE Let's hope not.

Silence.

RACHEL So, I'm here.

SUE Didn't think you'd miss the chance to share half an Embassy with me?

RACHEL Is that what we used to smoke?

SUE And voddy in the flask?

RACHEL With Kia-ora.

SUE "Just takin' a picnic up the woods, mum." *(Lifting her plastic cup)*

RACHEL Smirnoff?

SUE Tetley.

RACHEL What are we drinkin' to?

SUE Mates?

RACHEL Old mates. *(Silence)*

SUE I'm glad you've come, after Friday. *(Beat)* I was so effin rude.

RACHEL I'm not surprised, not sure I'd like some nosy beggar giving me a food parcel.

SUE It wasn't like that was it? *(Beat)* If things were t'other way round, I hope I'd do the same.

RACHEL Hope?

SUE I've never been as nice as you.

RACHEL Don't be soft.

SUE Don?

RACHEL That's water under the bridge in't it.

SUE It was a long time ago, if that's what you mean.

RACHEL All forgotten.

SUE He'll perhaps be changing his mind after all.

RACHEL What?

SUE He found the food.

RACHEL But how...

SUE The Sainsbury's bag. I didn't put it down far enough in the dustbin.

RACHEL HE was putting the rubbish out?

SUE A lot of the men are less shy of women's chores these days.

RACHEL Row?

SUE Terrible.

RACHEL I'm sorry.

SUE It's not your fault.

RACHEL Didn't think he'd find out?

SUE Deception's never been me strong point.

RACHEL That's true.

SUE I could've lied, but once you start with that.

Silence.

RACHEL So what now?

SUE Don't know. I've been sent to Coventry.

RACHEL Things are pretty tough down there.

SUE One in ten.

Beat.

You see Brenda?

RACHEL Yes.

Beat.

SUE And? *(Beat)*

RACHEL Alright. Actually she wer' very nice.

SUE Been round this one a couple a times. Seventy-two. Seventy-four.

RACHEL This one's different somehow.

SUE Yer not wrong there.

RACHEL I didn't tell Bob.

Beat. SUE *looks at her.*

About seeing you.

SUE What else didn't you tell 'im?

RACHEL What do you mean?

SUE Yer gunna sit 'ere and change subject?

RACHEL We're still talkin' about the same thing aren't we?

SUE Missin' stuff out.

Beat.

Like you gettin' arrested?

RACHEL She told you?

SUE Did you really think she wouldn't?

RACHEL I suppose I thought, I thought that, she wouldn't want you knowing she'd taken me, with me being/a scab's wife an all...

SUE Yer got yerself bloody arrested love, what were you thinkin'?

RACHEL I wanted to go and support what you was all doin' and Brenda thought I would only know if I went...and... I didn't get meself arrested on purpose... I just...was shakin'/the tin and—

SUE What were you thinkin', goin'? What if/

RACHEL I don't know. I don't know anything anymore. Everything I thought were solid is like quicksand.

Beat.

I wanted to, do something, and I wanted to fix things between you and me, and then, that happened. *(Beat)* I was proper terrified in that cell.

SUE It's not split trousers is it?

RACHEL It's a start.

SUE Not something you can fix. Until we win.

RACHEL I have to wait till then?

SUE I've already split you from one bloke.

RACHEL Nobody's talking about us splitting.

SUE There's at least two marriages on the rocks over this that I know about.

RACHEL You can't split a rock without a crack in it first.

SUE And if he catches on you've jumped sides?

RACHEL I haven't.

SUE Yet?

RACHEL *(she hesitates)* I'm on at lunchtime.

SUE Go on then.

Scene Three

The soup kitchen. Physical sequence. A **GROUP OF**
MINERS' *wives are packing food parcels with tins, baby*
food, sanitary towels, cereal, razors, jars of jam etc. Their
movements are stylized in a rhythmic routine. Filling and
passing, filling and passing, piling the filled boxes up into
a wall of boxes at the front of the stage.

Filling the boxes.

SHIRLEY Man, woman, one kiddie.

DERA Single man.

SHIRLEY Razors.

DERA Man, woman, two kiddies.

SUE Extra jam and eggs.

SHIRLEY Russian writing on this one.

SUE Serbian bean soup that.

DERA Three toilet rolls the day after.

SUE I keep mine fer throwin' at police.

Laughter.

BRENDA Man, woman, five kiddies.

DERA Nappies?

BRENDA We need extra.

SUE We'll get them somehow.

SHIRLEY Pram's broken.

BRENDA Old Minto'll fix it.

DERA Bedsheets needed in the prefabs.

SHIRLEY Someone wants a fire guard.

DERA Children's shoes.

SHIRLEY Men's trousers.

DERA Trouble with the bills in Bluebell Close.

SHIRLEY Number 37 again.

BRENDA Aye, hit the nail on the head.

SUE She left him you know.

BRENDA Who can blame her.

DERA Came back after three weeks.

SHIRLEY We're not snapped that easily.

> *One woman is having her box forcibly "unpacked" as if in a police search.*

DERA (**MALE POLICEMAN**'s *voice, throughout this sequence*) What's in the box?

SHIRLEY Just a few bits fer me family.

DERA Empty it out.

SHIRLEY It'll get dirty.

DERA Let me help you. (*Begins to take items and drop them on the floor, including emptying a pack of cornflakes*)

SHIRLEY Just a few bits fer me family, do you have to, officer?

DERA Where do they live?

SHIRLEY I don't have to tell you that.

DERA Where do they live?

SHIRLEY I'm just visiting me family. (**DERA** *as* **POLICE OFFICER** *picks up a bag of sanitary towels, puts them back, moves away*) What's the matter officer? (**SHIRLEY** *picks up the spilt items and puts them back in the box. The women are now moving the boxes into a wall of boxes at the front downstage centre*)

SUE European-style road blocks anywhere you want to travel.

BRENDA It's easier to get out of East Berlin than South Yorkshire.

DERA Where are you going?

SUE Just down to the shops.

DERA What is the purpose of your journey?

SUE To get some stuff in.

DERA I could charge you with breach of the peace.

SUE I'm only going to buy some dog food.

SHIRLEY Razor blades and toothpaste from London.

BRENDA £300 of food from Holland.

SHIRLEY Dover. Nappies and tampax.

DERA *(as herself from now on)* Thirty pound of meat.

SHIRLEY Two sacks of spuds.

DERA Two stone of frozen veg.

SHIRLEY Two gas rings. Three hundred dinners.

BRENDA No box contents worth more than £4.

SUE Or they'll have your supplementary benefit back off you.

BRENDA One hundred and fifty boxes to get done.

SUE I don't count sheep in bed no more, I count boxes.

  Laughter.

Scene Four

*The roundabout, 9.00pm, Wednesday evening. It has
just begun to get properly dark; the remaining light fades
during the scene. Car headlights approach and pass
illuminating* BETHANY *as she stands on the roadside, a
small rucksack on her back. This happens a few times,
she is waiting, still, she waits for a long time, as long as
possible, we think no-one is coming. Eventually* CHARLENE
runs in out of breath.

CHARLENE I couldn't get out.

BETHANY Bloody nora, I thought you weren't coming.

CHARLENE I had to wait till me dad had taken dog out.

BETHANY I wanted to get off before it got properly dark, just
before.

CHARLENE Get off where? Yer ages from the bus stop and the last
one's nine-thirty int'it?

BETHANY Not the bus. I'm going on the motorway, did you bring
everything?

CHARLENE *(unpacking a carrier bag as she speaks)* The mac's a
bit small, I haven't worn it in years. In whose car?

BETHANY It's fine.

CHARLENE How are you gettin' down the motorway? *(Taking out
the A-Z)* She'll be lookin' for it though fer Saturday.

BETHANY I'm gonna hitch. *(She produces a sign from behind
her, it is written on the back of a Coal Not Dole sign, it reads
LONDON)* Money, did you get money?

CHARLENE I managed to get a fiver out of the Christmas money,
but I have to put it back, she counts it, not every week, but she
counts it, you can't/

BETHANY I need to go.

CHARLENE To London? Why?

BETHANY I need to.

CHARLENE You mean, like running off? You could never do a runner, you hate roughing it, what about when the water got cut off, you made such a carry on/

BETHANY This is different, I can't stop, it's serious. *(She is frantically shoving everything into her bag)*

CHARLENE What is? What's happened?

BETHANY I didn't get to the...she/found...

CHARLENE The pictures, yer Aunty Brenda saw the pictures, that's it right?

BETHANY Yes.

CHARLENE It's just a picture of a copper, you can say you were spyin' on 'em.

BETHANY I can't, cos I wasn't, and its not.

CHARLENE Not what?

BETHANY Not, just a picture of 'im.

CHARLENE 'Im that yer soft on?

BETHANY It's 'im and me.

CHARLENE Yer what?

BETHANY 'Im and me in the pictures.

CHARLENE There's more than one? **(BETHANY** *nods)* Bloody 'ell.

BETHANY So I need to go to London. NOW.

CHARLENE Why London? You don't know anyone in London. *(Beat)* Him? But he's up here.

BETHANY He's not.

CHARLENE What?

BETHANY They've moved him, a lot of them, back for Saturday, fer the march.

CHARLENE Then that's it, isn't it, go on the coach on Saturday with the others and meet him. Or...you don't 'ave 'is address or 'owt.

BETHANY I do. And his number.

CHARLENE Fuckin' 'ell.

BETHANY Charlene!

CHARLENE What has actually happened? You betta not 'ave gone past first base? We said we'd say to each other if we was gunna, with a lad.

BETHANY This is different.

CHARLENE How is it bloody different, 'es a lad isn't 'e?

BETHANY Yes, but, don't be childish.

CHARLENE It's not me who's runnin' away is it.

BETHANY I'm not runnin' away. I am going to London.

CHARLENE Same difference.

BETHANY *begins to walk, we hear the sound of traffic increase,* CHARLENE *follows,* BETHANY *holds out her sign, sticks out her thumb.*

You can't do this. It's not safe.

BETHANY If you hadn't been late, I'd be half-way to London by now.

CHARLENE Not half-way, it takes hours.

BETHANY Shut up.

CHARLENE I don't see why you can't go on Saturday on the coach, I'll come with if yer like.

BETHANY *(almost shouting)* Because me Aunty Brenda has given me two days to "do the right thing" and tell me Mum, or she's threatening to tell me dad, which is MUCH worse. OK? OK?

CHARLENE Bloody 'ell.

BETHANY Right. Now piss off home before you get in bother an' all.

CHARLENE Call me. You've got change 'ave yer?

BETHANY I've got change.

Scene Five

Physical sequence. The women are making a banner, unrolling a long piece of cloth on two poles and sticking already embroidered and decorated pieces onto it, including the words "WOMEN IN ACTION" At the end of the dialogue they hold up the banner and march off. Their voices match those of the people whose words they embody.

TWO YORKSHIRE MINERS' WIVES *and* **TWO WELSH MINERS' WIVES.**

WELSH MW 1 Take me on the picket line son.

WELSH MW 2 That's not a place I want my mum.

WELSH MW 1 Take me on the picket line son.

WELSH MW 2 That's not a place I want my mum.

WELSH MW 1 Take me.

WELSH MW 2 Can't. The car is full.

WELSH MW 1 Take me!

WELSH MW 2 It's not safe.

WELSH MW 1 Take me!

WELSH MW 2 They don't care who they hit.

WELSH MW 1 I'm coming.

WELSH MW 2 I'm proud of you, Mum.

YORKS MW 1 I used to have my nets down every two weeks.

YORKS MW 2 Only get them down now if they was in tatters.

YORKS MW 1 Hoover through every morning.

YORKS MW 2 No time for that now.

YORKS MW 1 I used to ask if I wanted to go somewhere.

YORKS MW 2 On a trip. Up the club.

YORK MW 1 Now I tell him.

YORKS MW 2 When am I going to get my mum back? The one I had before the strike?

YORKS MW 1 She's gone flying.

WELSH MW 1 The doctor told me, the miners' strike was affecting my nerves. I told her it was the police and the government affecting my nerves.

WELSH MW 2 You don't see us on the telly, but we are there.

WELSH MW 1 This time last year I was doing the washing up.

WELSH MW 2 We haven't come here to beg for food, but to fight for a cause.

WELSH MW 1 Four times I've been down London, never seen the sights any time.

YORKS MW 1 They fined a lass fer throwin' eggs at a lorry.

YORKS MW 2 But never found who threw the brick that killed 'er son.

WELSH MW 1 What's the difference between The Sun and The Beano.

ALL Four p.

WELSH MW 2 How many of Britain's seventeen national newspapers printed the picture of the truncheon attack on a young woman at Orgreave?

ALL One.

WELSH MW 1 You won't get me stuck back in that house now I've seen the horizon.

WELSH MW 2 Once you know what life can be, you're not going to pop back in that box now are you?

Scene Six

Thursday 9th August, 5am. Outside SUE's *house, we hear a car door slam.* BETHANY *walks up to the house, she is reluctant to enter, she sits on the step. A few minutes pass, she shivers.The door opens,* DON *comes out, steps over her and lights a cigarette, stands in front of her.*

DON So what's all this about lass?

BETHANY Nowt.

DON You come home at five in the morning and it's nowt.

BETHANY I was stoppin' at a mate's. It's nowt. Didn't think you'd notice.

DON I've noticed.

BETHANY That'll be first time since strike started then.

DON I don't need yer lip.

BETHANY I might of needed a bit of attention.

DON You've got it.

BETHANY I said I might've needed it, not that I need it now, right now. I'm OK right now.

DON OK are you?

BETHANY Yes thanks.

DON And 'appen I'm not. *(Beat.* BETHANY *turns away from him)* When a daughter of mine is found trying to hitch a lift at the motorway junction in the middle of the night.

BETHANY How do you know/

DON Scotty rang me when they dropped 'im off, you must've known they'd tell me.

BETHANY It's the morning not the night.

DON   Don't split hairs.

BETHANY   It's nowt.

DON   You said. *(Beat)* If you're trying to hitch down to London, it must be summat.

BETHANY   Leave it, Dad.

DON   I can't though can I?

BETHANY   You could.

DON   Don't be flippant young lady.

BETHANY   I'm sixteen, I could get married if I wanted to.

DON   And who would you be marrying, lady?

BETHANY   Nobody, I'm just sayin' I'm not a kid no more.

DON   Don't behave like one then.

BETHANY   I'm not.

DON   Runnin' away.

BETHANY   I wasn't runnin' away, I was going somewhere.

DON   Now, we're getting' to it.

> *Beat.*

Is there some boy involved? Scotty said one of the lads saw you up near the Coach and Horses.

BETHANY   Why would I be up there, it's a pigs' pub. *(Beat)* Must be someone else.

DON   You've not been up there?

BETHANY   I'm underage remember.

DON   Not a kid anymore you just said.

BETHANY   I'm not, but I'm not old enough to get in the pub now am I.

DON   If I find out you're lying to me.

BETHANY   What? What are you gonna do if you find out I'm lying?

DON   There'll be some bother.

BETHANY Bother like what you did to Mum.

DON What are you on about?

BETHANY Like what you was doin' to Mum. Is that what yer gonner do?

DON Bethany?

BETHANY *(shouting)* You think I didn't see, but I did. I see things, and hear things.

DON It wer' nothin'. An argument.

BETHANY Didn't look like nothing to me. *(Standing)* Can I go in now? *(She opens the door)* And can you tell your mates to stop spyin' on me, it's bloody creepy.

She goes in. **DON** *is left standing. He lights another cigarette. Blackout.*

Scene Seven

Friday 10th August, morning. BRENDA*'s kitchen.* SUE *and* BRENDA *are making final "battle plans" for the march the next day. They have a map of the route, placards and badges laid out on the table. They are sorting through everything as they speak, ticking things off etc.*

SUE I'm still not convinced you should be going.

BRENDA I'm going if it kills me.

SUE I don't want it to kill you, that's what I'm mithered about.

BRENDA Don't be mithered.

SUE How can I not be, you've had a few health scares too many in the last month.

BRENDA As long as I don't get meself arrested this time, I can keep it calm, just walk along with the rest of the girls. I can't miss this. It's what we've been working up to.

SUE You've done the lion's share of the work.

BRENDA I'm the one with time on me hands.

SUE Knitting? Gardening?

BRENDA Not when our community's being smashed to pieces right left and centre. There'll be nothing left to knit for. *(Going through a list)* So, all the places are taken on the coach now?

SUE A couple backed out and I've filled them up.

BRENDA I can see. *(Looking at the list)* Our Bethany?

SUE And her mate.

BRENDA They weren't put off the last time then?

SUE Seems not. Her dad thinks it'll take her mind off things.

BRENDA What things exactly?

SUE Oh, nothing, just teenage stuff.

BRENDA I thought you weren't speakin'?

SUE Me and Bethany?

BRENDA You and Don, you know full well/who I meant.

SUE Who told you?

BRENDA Common knowledge.

SUE Course.

BRENDA You sorted it then?

SUE Patched over the cracks, we'll see how things are when this is over.

BRENDA You can't postpone life.

SUE I'm postponing this bit, too much else to be done.

BRENDA And Bethany? *(SUE doesn't answer)* She in a spot of bother?

SUE What makes you say that?

BRENDA Teenage trouble?

SUE You remember what we got up to.

BRENDA All sorts. *(Beat)* Boy trouble?

SUE Nooo, no, I don't think so. She...one of the lads, one of Don's lads found her up on the slip road by the bypass, tryin' to hitch a lift to London. Luckily no-one picked her up...until they came along.

BRENDA They picked her up?

SUE Course, Scotty, brought her back home with 'er tail between 'er legs.

BRENDA Why London?

SUE It's the obvious place fer runnin' in't it?

BRENDA So now yer takin' her on Saturday.

SUE Yes. *(Beat)* She'll be with us, get it out of her system.

BRENDA I hope yer right.

SUE It's getting to us all different ways in't it.

BRENDA Hmm.

SUE I'm not really givin' 'em enough attention, leavin' 'em to fend fer therselves a lot.

BRENDA They're not kiddies anymore.

SUE They're not, but all the same.

BRENDA We'll've achieved something by the end of tomorrow. Quite a feat. All the support from down South, unbelievable.

SUE What's the plan for if we lose someone?

BRENDA Everyone has instructions how to get to Burgess Park and meet us back there, next to the Co-op tea hut.

SUE And the minibuses.

BRENDA For the kiddies? Yes, it's all planned, they're being taken down to the crèche from the beginning of the march. I'm not too sure about givin' out the 'In Case Of Arrest' paper.

SUE We 'ave to, you know yerself, what can 'appen.

BRENDA That's it in't it. I'm used to the possibility. It'll be a shock fer most of them to even think it could happen.

SUE Still.

BRENDA We have to give it out.

SUE Better start on these teacakes fer the coach.

BRENDA Won't butter themselves. *(Grabbing a bag of teacakes and beginning to butter them)* I'm glad the girls are coming, marching to the Palace to make our case, it's something they'll remember fer a lifetime. *(They butter in silence)* And don't be blaming yerself, there'll always be enough people blamin'...

SUE Blamin' meself fer what?

BRENDA Bethany. Anything to do with the kids. You've been a good mum, you are a good mum.

SUE It's not fer me to say.

BRENDA Don't see why not. It's definitely fer me to say. *(Beat)* Flasks?

SUE Next to the sink in bag, got every flask in't village I think, I'll rinse 'em when we're done with this.

BRENDA No tea, no marchin'. *(They laugh)*

Scene Eight

Saturday 11th August 6am. The women are on a coach down to London for the start of the women's march. BETHANY *and* CHARLENE *are sat near the rear of the coach. We hear general chatter and possibly singing, a few children's voices.*

CHARLENE I feel sick.

BETHANY You do not, we only just set off.

CHARLENE I hate motorways.

BETHANY Depends where yer goin'.

CHARLENE Suppose.

BETHANY And you were the one that wanted to come anyroad.

CHARLENE If we were goin' to Michael.

BETHANY Yer bessie mate MJ.

CHARLENE Bog off.

Beat.

You didn't get a lift then the other night?

BETHANY You know I didn't, don't bloody rub it in.

CHARLENE I told yer this was a better idea at the start.

BETHANY Alright, clever clogs.

CHARLENE 'Ow are yer plannin' to find 'im, there'll be load of 'em there and they all look the same. Pink porky faces.

BETHANY He is not porky.

CHARLENE Didn't mean HIM, anyhow, I've not seen 'im close, he could be a right minger with bad breath.

BETHANY He has mints.

CHARLENE Oh does he now, pops one in before you get to it does he?

BETHANY You make it sound so crude, it's, it's...

CHARLENE Like "Our Tune", all mushy, what is your tune?

BETHANY Stop it. (CHARLENE *pulls faces*) Stop it.

CHARLENE You have one don't you, ooo let me guess... 'Total Eclipse Of The Heart'. (BETHANY *punches her in the arm*) 'Temptation'. *(She sings the title)*

BETHANY It's not a joke, it's serious.

CHARLENE OK. *(Beat)* Tell me then?

BETHANY It's 'Hello'.

CHARLENE Oh, my, God. That is so cheesy.

BETHANY What's the point of me sayin' if yer just going to be stupid.

Beat.

CHARLENE Sorry. *(Beat)* So where are you meeting him?

BETHANY His station is not that far from the rally thing, the end of the march. He's on an early so he thinks they'll let him off by then, by when the march might get to the park.

CHARLENE *(looking at instructions on a piece of paper, a route)* Burgess Park.

BETHANY Yeah, it's south of the river, near where his station is.

CHARLENE And what, yer just going to go there? And then what?

Beat.

Yer not stayin'? Yer can't stay?

BETHANY I don't know, I, I, just said I'd see him.

CHARLENE And then come back?

BETHANY I don't know.

CHARLENE And I'm hangin' about waitin' for you. You still haven't told me what's gone on. First of all you just said you fancied 'im, and then there was all this photo mystery. I mean, which base have you got to, I mean, how far on is it?

BETHANY Yer bein' bloody crude again.

CHARLENE I am not, you 'ave to tell somebody.

BETHANY I don't HAVE to.

CHARLENE Right.

BETHANY *gets a puzzle book and biro out of her bag and opens it.* **CHARLENE** *looks out of the window.*

BETHANY Second.

Scene Nine

Midday the same day. The heart of the women's march.
There is a constant hum of sound, footsteps and chanting,
the chanting intersects with individual lines. It is as if we
are watching the whole march and hearing the thoughts
of what the strike had cost the women and their families.
There is no silence until the dropping of the black poppies.

ALL (*singing to the tune of "BREAD OF HEAVEN"*)
COAL FOR BRITAIN. COAL FOR BRITAIN. DON'T PUT MINERS ON
THE DOLE. (ON THE DOLE) DON'T PUT MINERS ON THE DOLE.

YORKS MW 1
MAGGIE, MAGGIE, MAGGIE.

ALL
OUT OUT OUT.

YORKS MW 1
MAGGIE, MAGGIE, MAGGIE.

ALL
OUT, OUT, OUT.

YORKS MW 1
MAGGIE.

ALL
OUT.

YORKS MW 1
MAGGIE.

ALL
OUT.

YORKS MW 1
MAGGIE, MAGGIE, MAGGIE.

ALL
OUT. OUT. OUT.

COAL NOT DOLE, COAL NOT DOLE.

Cont underneath this dialogue.

SUE Why are we not rallying in Jubilee Gardens?

BRENDA There's a rally fer Donald Duck's birthday, takes precedent.

SUE That's Mickey Mouse policing for you.

ALL Women against pit closures. Women against pit closures *(x 3)*.

SUE It's not just us, that's what I can't get over, the people from here, the local unions.

BRENDA It's all the visits and the planning, it's us, the women, all of us women north and south, we made this happen.

YORKS MW 1 Maggie, Maggie, Maggie.

ALL Out, out, out.

YORKS MW 1 Maggie, Maggie, Maggie.

ALL Out, out, out.

YORKS MW 1 Maggie.

ALL Out.

YORKS MW 1 Maggie.

ALL Out.

YORKS MW 1 Maggie, Maggie, Maggie.

ALL Out. Out. Out.

SCOTTS MW 1 Electric's been cut off.

SCOTTS MW 2 50p meter.

ALL Women against pit closures.

YORKS MW 2 We're the real Iron Ladies.

Laughter.

ALL Women against pit closures.

WELSH MW 1 Not paid the milkman since February.

WELSH MW 2 Sat indoors, nothing to eat for three days.

SUE *(singing to tune of "DRUNKEN SAILOR")*
WHAT DO WE WANT?

ALL *(singing to same tune)*
COAL NOT DOLE.

SUE *(singing to tune of "DRUNKEN SAILOR")*
WHAT DO WE WANT?

ALL *(singing to same tune)*
COAL NOT DOLE.

SUE *(singing to tune of "DRUNKEN SAILOR")*
WHAT DO WE WANT?

ALL *(singing to same tune)*
COAL NOT DOLE. KEEP THE PITS OPEN.

BRENDA No biscuits or sweets fer the kiddies.

YORK MW 1 Cashed in the insurance.

YORKS MW 2 Sold the car.

SUE Washin' me hair with washing up liquid.

WELSH MW 1 I'm not going to cry. I'm going picketing.

SUE *(singing to tune of "DRUNKEN SAILOR")*
WHAT DO WE WANT?

ALL *(singing to same tune)*
JOBS NOT JAIL.

SUE *(singing to tune of "DRUNKEN SAILOR")*
WHAT DO WE WANT?

ALL *(singing to same tune)*
JOBS NOT JAIL.

SUE *(singing to tune of "DRUNKEN SAILOR")*
WHAT DO WE WANT?

ALL *(singing to same tune)*
JOBS NOT JAIL. KEEP THE PITS OPEN.
Save our pits. Save our pits.

WELSH MW 1 I'm thinkin' of joinin' the party.

WELSH MW 2 They 'aven't the strength to knock the skin off a rice puddin'.

WELSH MW 1 I gotta do somethin'.

ALL Save our pits. Save our pits. Save our pits. Save our pits.

SUE Past the Palace.

BRENDA Hand in our petition.

WELSH MW 1 "We the women of the British Mining Communities—"

SCOTTS MW 1 "Appeal for your support in our struggle—"

YORKS MW 1 "To hold together the very lives of our communities—"

The next three lines build and overlap.

Coal not dole.

SUE Save our communities.

SCOTTS MW 1 Jobs not jail.

ALL *(to the tune of "DRUNKEN SAILOR")*
WORK TILL YOU DIE.

Cont...building.
STRIKE TILL YOU WIN.

Cont...building.

This chant builds to a crescendo silence.

SUE Downing Street. The singing and chanting stops. Silence. Black flowers in memory of the lads who died at Ollerton.

The women take black petals or flowers from inside their pockets etc and throw them centre stage onto the floor. A single child-like voice begins to sing "SIX JOLLY MINERS", this continues quietly underneath to the end of the scene. The march passes by SUE *as she speaks, swoops around her, draws her forward, until she is left alone.*

Down the Walworth Road, it seems like we've been marchin' from Jarrow, some off us 'ave come from there of course, not on foot, fit to drop, and people, just people comin' out of shops and places along the road and clappin' an' cheerin' and the DHSS workers throw a banner out of their office window. So many women, and I'm laughin' and cryin' all together. *(Beat)* And then I go cold, like ice runnin' down me back, when did I last see our Bethany?

Scene Ten

We hear the sound of a brass band and a protest band playing on a stage, women calling to each other, they weave in and out of one another, waving, carrying rolled up banners and slightly battered placards. The following sequence can be played as a "round" ebbing and flowing.

YORKS MW 1 What a day.

SCOTTS MW 1 What a day.

YORKS MW 2 How many of us do you think?

YORKS MW 1 They're saying twenty-three thousand.

YORKS MW 2 Twenty-three thousand.

SCOTTS MW 2 Twenty-three thousand, did you hear that?

WELSH MW 1 Enough cakes now David, I don't want you sick on the coach home.

WELSH MW 2 Do you know where we pick up the coach?

WELSH MW 1 It's on the piece of paper they gave us.

WELSH MW 2 I lost that ages ago.

WELSH MW 1 Someone'll 'ave one, just ask, they're a friendly bunch.

Through this crowd of women **BETHANY** *is running, directionless, she is still running, tears streaming down her face, out of breath. We see* **BRENDA** *looking for her, they are separated, they cannot see each other. Eventually* **BRENDA** *spots someone she thinks is* **BETHANY**.

BRENDA *(shouting)* Bethany, Bethany, Bethany.

BETHANY sees BRENDA and runs in the opposite direction, **SUE** *appears from the crowd and grabs hold of her.*

BETHANY No, no, no, no, no, no, no/no, no...

SUE Bethany love, where are you going, who are you running from/what's happened, what is it...

BETHANY I can't, I can't, no, no, just let me get on't coach and, I just want to go back 'ome/no, no...

SUE and BRENDA are struggling to keep her still, finally she sags to the floor pulling them down with her.

I'm sorry Aunty Brenda, is yer skirt dirty?

BRENDA Never mind about that, are you alright, has something happened to you.

BETHANY Nothing has happened/I...

SUE Are you hurt? Who hurt you? What happened?

BETHANY Nothing, nothing, he didn't, nobody hurt me.

SUE He? He who?/Who?

BRENDA Let 'er speak, it's best she gets it out herself.

SUE Gets what out, what's going on? Do you know something/ I don't? He?

BETHANY *(speaking rapidly, out of breath)* I went to meet someone...he... I didn't get to...it wasn't...

SUE He? He?

BRENDA Let her get it out.

SUE Get what out. WHAT IS THIS ABOUT?

BRENDA She's tellin' you, will you/just let her speak...

SUE Where were you goin' love?

BETHANY There was a bus stop and I sat on the seats and lots of buses went by, lots. A lady with...she had lots of beads in her hair, she asked me where I was going and I said Burgess Park because I remembered that, and she crossed me over the road put me on the bus and said, get off when you see the park, and I got off when I saw the park and I started running again.

SUE OK, I am still none the wiser lady, what is going on?

BRENDA Go on love.

BETHANY Aunty Brenda I can't. I feel stupid.

BRENDA You are not stupid at all, but you must say, we agreed. *(Turning to* **SUE***)* We agreed that I wouldn't tell you about this, if she did, I wanted to give her time to do the right thing.

SUE Going running off in bloody London, is the right thing?

BRENDA She's doing the right thing now, aren't you pet?

BETHANY *(quietly)* I've been seein' a copper, Mum.

BRENDA I told her I'd tell her father if she didn't tell you.

SUE What were you thinkin'? He's nearly at breakin' point, this 'ull finish him.

BETHANY I don't know.

SUE What copper?

BRENDA Do you not remember being sixteen?

SUE What copper, where did you meet a copper?

BRENDA There's one 'round every corner at the moment.

SUE She wouldn't be speakin' to them though?

BRENDA She obviously did, or we wouldn't be talkin' about it.

SUE Seein'? A copper? Why a copper?

BRENDA Curiosity? Money?

SUE What are you sayin'?

BRENDA Not that, let's not/

SUE From the town? Not/one of them.

BRENDA Yes.

BETHANY *(standing)* Will you both stop talkin' about me, I am here. *(Beat)* And I do get it. It's not best idea to go out with someone on t'other side in any war, I thought he was different and he wasn't and now I feel stupid. Alright?

SUE How long has this been going on?

BETHANY Just since the beginning of the holidays.

SUE ALL summer.

BETHANY It's a couple of weeks.

SUE More than a couple.

BETHANY I was bored, there's no money to do owt, I was hangin' about/at the gates...

SUE And havin' a carry on with a pig was the way to fix that.

BETHANY I didn't do it on purpose it just sort of happened.

SUE How do you just sort of happen to find yerself with a/

BETHANY Pig. *(SUE opens her mouth)* You said it. I don't know. He offered to buy me a drink up the pub and *(beat)* I wanted to go for a drink up the pub and no other bugger 'ad any money.

SUE DO NOT SWEAR.

BETHANY Bugger isn't buggering swearing.

BRENDA I think that's enough isn't it. It's not happening any more, she feels ashamed, that's enough.

SUE She doesn't sound very ashamed to me.

BRENDA Sue.

SUE starts to walk in the direction of the coach.

You are too stiff sometimes. Yes, have principles, but you wear them like sunglasses and you can't see when someone wants to change their mind. Rachel might've come today if she weren't so perishing frightened of you.

SUE *(turns)* So I'm to blame for scabs not turning AND me daughter at it with a white shirt. I'm glad we've sorted that one.

BRENDA Sue. Sue...

She walks off. BRENDA follows with BETHANY behind her.

Scene Eleven

CHARLENE *is leaning on the back of the coach, she is smoking.* BETHANY *appears round the side of the coach,* CHARLENE *jumps, hurriedly stubbing out the cigarette before realising it is her friend.*

CHARLENE Thought you weren't coming back wi' us?

BETHANY I never said that.

CHARLENE Thought you were emigrating to London.

BETHANY You don't emigrate to London.

CHARLENE Did he ask you to stay.

BETHANY No. Shall we just get on and wait. Me feet are killin'.

CHARLENE You didn't see him did you?

BETHANY *(scowls)*

CHARLENE Did you get lost and have to come back? If it'd been me, I'd've got proper lost, I've no sense of direction me.

BETHANY I didn't get lost.

CHARLENE You did see him?

BETHANY Yes, I saw him.

Silence.

CHARLENE It's like pullin' teeth this.

BETHANY I saw him.

CHARLENE And...

BETHANY I was just watchin' 'im, standing on the wall laughin' gabbin' to 'is mates, he had his helmet in his hand and his hair was... like he'd just taken it off... I didn't call out... I wanted to. I dunno...they were laughin' at a story about pullin' a woman

70

up a bank and leavin' 'er with 'er drawers all showin' and sayin' "she got what she deserved", "she got what she deserved" and he were laughin', and sayin' "we didn't need a dog to herd them 'cows' and I couldn't stop listening…like I had to hear it all, all of it, but it didn't stop, it went on and on, and 'im and 'is mate bragging about what they'd done "on the front line", like it wer' a film or summat.

CHARLENE You just stood there.

BETHANY Yeah.

CHARLENE Did he see you?

BETHANY Yeah.

CHARLENE And?

BETHANY Yeah. He saw me.

CHARLENE And?

BETHANY I didn't say anything.

CHARLENE Now what?

BETHANY Go home and face the music. Aunty Brenda made me tell me mum.

CHARLENE Hell's bells.

BETHANY She thinks it's finished.

CHARLENE Isn't it?

BETHANY He shouted me, I don't know what he shouted, I'd started running, I didn't know where I was running, I just knew it was the only thing I wanted to do, just run.

CHARLENE Did he run after yer?

BETHANY I didn't turn round.

CHARLENE So?

BETHANY He can't call me. I'd have to call him. I got his number in the section house.

CHARLENE Will yer?

BETHANY I know what he thinks of us now.

CHARLENE You don't know what he thinks of you?

BETHANY I am one of the "cows" though aren't I?

CHARLENE He won't have meant you, will 'e?

BETHANY Is it like me mum says, class war?

CHARLENE Then he should be on the same side.

BETHANY He's not though is he?

CHARLENE None of this makes any sense to me any more. *(Beat)* Will she tell yer dad?

BETHANY I doubt it. She's never in long enough.

CHARLENE Right.

BETHANY I'd be letting her down if I call him.

CHARLENE I did say it were a shit idea.

BETHANY I'm getting on, you coming?

> **BETHANY** *goes round the side of the coach to get on.*

CHARLENE I did say.

Scene Twelve

BRENDA's *kitchen Sunday 12th August.* BRENDA *and* RACHEL *sit around the table. A plate of uneaten toast and a full mug of tea sits in front of* RACHEL. *The atmosphere is tense.*

Silence.

There is a knock at the door. SUE *enters.*

SUE So. I've not really been to bed, unless you count puttin' me pyjamas on, stickin' me cold feet onto Don and runnin' straight back downstairs to answer the piggin' phone. What's so urgent?

BRENDA It wasn't summat I could discuss on't phone.

SUE I see.

BRENDA Found her on't doorstep when I got back from the coach.

SUE Right.

RACHEL He asked me to leave.

SUE And yer did?

RACHEL Well, I came here. I haven't actually left.

SUE But yer did.

RACHEL He's asked me to decide.

BRENDA It's not just you that needs to do that.

RACHEL You were all for taking me on a picket and getting me to make me mind up.

BRENDA Make both yer minds up.

RACHEL Are you only interested in me being in if I can turn Bob?

BRENDA I didn't say that.

RACHEL He won't have his kids losing out.

SUE But he doesn't mind losing you?

RACHEL He hasn't lost me.

BRENDA Just because yer didn't pack a toothbrush.

RACHEL I didn't pack anything.

BRENDA But you did walk out when he asked?

RACHEL I told him I was coming here.

BRENDA He'd be thrilled about that.

RACHEL I'm not leaving me kids.

SUE Looks like yer just did/

BRENDA That's how he'll see it.

RACHEL What do you want? You want me to pick a side, and as soon as I try to/

BRENDA There are consequences to choosing.

RACHEL Don't you think I know that? He asked me to go. He didn't mean it.

SUE I wouldn't be too sure.

RACHEL I don't get it, you want me to join you and then you don't.

SUE 'Women against pit closures' can hardly have the wife of a lad who goes through those gates every day.

RACHEL You wanted me to do this.

SUE I didn't want you walking away from another husband.

RACHEL That's bloody cruel and bloody unfair.

SUE Bloody true though.

RACHEL Perhaps if you hadn't taken me fiancé off me.

SUE He wasn't your fiancé.

RACHEL He was about to be. I had to settle for that/bastard.

SUE You can't pin that on me. It was me that/

RACHEL Took me in, yes, you took me in, so you could be the one with all the answers, on top as usual, lady bloody bountiful, "stay as long as yer like...d'yer mind lookin' after the kiddies while we go up the club fer an hour", suited you down to the ground, more like. "Poor Rachel".

BRENDA This isn't helping.

RACHEL What if he still held a torch? Did you think of that, you all busy with Robbie and Bethany and me in me Wranglers, do you remember them, fit me like a glove them jeans, "You still look like a teenager Rach", he said to me. Do you remember? Do you? The barbeque...it was hot that summer.

BRENDA Stop it Rachel.

RACHEL Ever since school, egging me on and then changing the rules, getting us to all go out in a gang so you could whisper in 'is ear when I wasn't lookin'.

SUE He's always liked both of us.

RACHEL But you can't have two wives can you. You won, and you want to win now.

SUE What do you want Rachel, why have you come?

RACHEL To join the campaign. Proper.

SUE You're expecting us to take you in?

RACHEL He'll let me back in once he's cooled off.

SUE So, you'll go back to the scab and come and stir soup during the day. The women'll not stand fer that. One toe in the water and the other on dry land.

RACHEL They can hang onto their bloody urn. Nothing can stop me coming on the picket.

BRENDA The committee decides who goes in the mini-bus.

RACHEL I can drive meself if I want to.

SUE In the car paid for by his wages.

RACHEL So yer sayin, I've to keep away unless I can bring Bob out. Is that it? *(Beat) (To* **BRENDA***)* Why take me? Why?

BRENDA It was you that came to find me, came round to Sue's weren't it?

RACHEL I couldn't just do nothing.

SUE You could of.

RACHEL But I didn't.

Silence.

RACHEL So you win again. Come wi' us, join us, come on't march. But only if yer can make him fall in line.

BRENDA Don't know how to unpick this one.

SUE So you roped me in.

BRENDA You were in already. *(Beat)* You're right Rachel, We can't stop you comin' out, but do you really want to throw everything else over to join us?

RACHEL If pit goes in the closures, he's only sure of keeping it all afloat till that happens. It's shaky ground he's clingin' to.

SUE You said that to 'im did yer?

RACHEL Not in those exact words no, but we did have words, obviously.

BRENDA How did he find out?

RACHEL I told him. I decided to tell him. I didn't like going behind his back.

SUE Brave.

RACHEL You think?

BRENDA Or naïve.

RACHEL Thanks.

SUE *(letting out an exhausted sigh)* Why don't we sleep on it?

BRENDA You best go back right now. You did come with yer key?

RACHEL Of course. *(Beat)* You're not giving me an answer then?

SUE Brenda's right. We can't stop you, but...

BRENDA You know what's at stake. *(Beat)*

RACHEL I do.

SUE *(taking a slice of the cold toast and biting)* You might not need this, but I'm bloody famished.

Scene Thirteen

Two months later an awareness and fundraising meeting in Ruskin College Student Union. A packed hall with a hubbub of expectant chatter. BRENDA *slowly climbs onto a small wooden platform, her breath is laboured, we can see that the weeks of the dispute have taken their toll. She shuffles her notes, holds onto the lectern, the room quietens, she breathes in.*

BRENDA I would like to begin by thanking Ruskin College student protest committee for inviting us down *(beat)* for inviting us down *(she is breathing heavily, sweating)* thanking Ruskin College for inviting us, for inviting us... *(She sways, the audience shuffles uncomfortably)* We are already indebted to you for the parcels you have sent up and for the box of warm clothes, we, we... *(She clutches at the lectern, closes her eyes)* Thanking Ruskin College for inviting...

We hear the scrape of a chair and see RACHEL *walk from the back of the hall, her pace quickens during* BRENDA*'s last words, she reaches the lectern and holds her aunt by the shoulders, sits her down on the chair behind her and takes her place at the lectern.*

Invii... Inviting, Ruskin College...

There is a long silence, RACHEL *looks around the room, opens and shuts her mouth.*

RACHEL My Aunty Brenda is the strongest woman I know. *(She turns,* BRENDA *smiles.* RACHEL *gives her the glass of water from the lectern)* The truth is...um...she's um...worn out. *(Beat.* RACHEL *scrabbles in her head for words)* She's been out on the picket line nearly every day and getting up at the crack of dawn to work in the soup kitchen... *(She turns round to look at* BRENDA, *seeking inspiration)* There is not one home in my community that has not benefited from her support.

Beat.

I've never spoken like this, on a microphone, or to anybody, any more people than a room, but, well, there's a first time for everything. There would be people in my community who would say, "who does she think she is?"*(Pause)* I'm not a Miss World contestant or flippin' Yoko Ono, just a miner's wife, and a bloody scab one at that, who wants me on board? Getting up here to speak...and they'd be right. I am supporting the strike, well, I have been since August, but my husband is a scab. *(There is a murmur in the room)* I took vows, I am not going back on those. I can't change his mind, but I could change mine. You invited us down here and we came because you wanted to hear our story. My story isn't the one you were expecting, but I am telling it you all the same.

Her voice begins to rise in strength and power, she surprises herself as her her passion takes over.

I went to have a look for meself, instead of sittin' at home and watchin' it on the telly... I went out flying for meself, a flying picket, and what I saw *(pause)* it were like a war zone not a protest. I got meself arrested for the crime of asking the women of Nottingham to get their men out. They strip searched me *(murmuring)* and I thought, well, if they're going to this much trouble then there must be right on our side. I want to tell you about some of the things I've seen. Women and kiddies being punched and kicked, arrested for just pickin' coal off the stack to try and keep warm.

If we don't support the miners now, we are losing our future. It's not just the mines that will go, but our ability to defend workers' rights, ordinary decent people's rights, the right to work and put food on the table. The right to stand up for how we are treated. I don't know about you, but I don't want to be treated any old how. It's not just about this strike, it's about a lot of things that we can put our neb into, hospital closures, women's education, peace.

I believe Mrs Thatcher hoped this strike would divide the people of the South from the people of the North, but it won't, because we WON'T LET IT. WE ARE WOMEN WITH A VOICE AND WE WILL NOT BE SILENCED.

PROPERTY LIST

Metal Dustbin (Could be on set list)
Multiple cans of food 1980's labels/labels from Europe.(Alternative cans with no labels)
Large catering cans of food.
Two Sainsbury's bags circa 1980 (shopping for inside these bags, most not seen)
A fresh peach.
Chocolate Digestive biscuits. McVities 1980's
Notebook and biro (Bethany personal prop)
Packet of cigarettes, 1980's brand.
Bowl and spoon.
Placards (Women Against Pit Closures/Coal Not Dole etc)
A hammer/Nails.
4 metal dustbin lids for shields (or short round police shields/ depending on designer's choice)
Four wooden rolling pins (or police batons, depending on designer's choice)
Three Police Helmets (Costume/props)
Camera with several rolls of film 1980's
Mixing bowl
Wooden Spoon
Metal Saucepans.
Metal Spoons.
Metal Colander.
Printed Women Against Pit Closures leaflets.
Collecting Tin (Women Against Pit Closures).
A-Z book 1980's
Sleeping Bag.
Plastic Mac
Rucksack
1980's coins for telephone box
Drink flask 1980's
Carboard boxes for packing boxes scene. 1980's or plain.
Cloth banner for March and sewing scene (Could be on set list)
Clipboard with paper lists.
Cigarettes.

THIS
IS
NOT
THE
END

Lightning Source UK Ltd.
Milton Keynes UK
UKOW06f1459270817
308023UK00001B/10/P